Holy Ghost Holiday Help

365 Volume 1

Valencia Clark

REJOICE
Essential Publishing

Valencia Clark/Rejoice Essential Publishing

PO BOX 512

Effingham, SC 29541

www.republishing.org

Unless otherwise indicated, scripture is taken from the King James Version.'

Holy Ghost Holiday Help 365 Volume 1/Valencia Clark

ISBN-13: 978-1-956775-83-9

Dedication

I dedicate this book to Holy Spirit, my best friend.

Table of Contents

Foreword

In the chaos and commercialization surrounding holidays, it is easy to lose sight of the essence and significance of these special times. As Christians, our faith holds a central place in our lives, and we must approach these holidays with a focus on the spiritual rather than the material.

"*Holy Ghost Holiday Help 365 Volume 1*" is a compelling book that reminds us of the importance of celebrating our Christian faith with purpose and intentionality. Through its pages, Valencia illuminates the beauty of our religious traditions and provides practical guidance on infusing our celebrations with deep meaning while overcoming difficulties during the holiday season.

Drawing from biblical teachings, personal experiences, and historical context, *"Holy Ghost Holiday Help 365 Volume 1"* guides us to dig deeper into the rich spiritual significance of the holiday. Exploring the biblical trust and spiritual tool reminded all that no matter the season, Jesus still holds the transformative power of these holy moments.

This book offers a refreshing perspective on celebrating with purpose, emphasizing the importance of gratitude, fellowship, and acts of service. It challenges us to examine our motivations for celebrating and encourages us to align our actions with the teachings of Christ. Valencia's heartfelt storytelling and practical suggestions allow us to create meaningful traditions that draw us closer to God and impact those around us.

Through thought-provoking questions and guided reflections, *"Holy Ghost Holiday Help 365 Volume 1"* invites us to reexamine our priorities during the holiday season. It encourages us to slow down, seek solitude, and engage in personal reflection—creating space for Holy Spirit to guide and renew our hearts. This book is a gentle reminder that our celebrations can be a time of spiritual growth, personal transformation, and deepening our relationship with God.

The beauty of *"Holy Ghost Holiday Help 365 Volume 1"* lies in its ability to bridge the gap between our faith traditions and everyday lives. It reminds us that our Christian identity is not limited to a single day of worship but should permeate every aspect of our existence. By infusing our daily practices with the principles of love, compassion, and humility, we can live out our faith in a way that honors Christ and inspires those around us.

As you embark on this journey through *"Holy Ghost Holiday Help 365 Volume 1,"* I implore you to approach each page with an open heart and a willingness to let Holy Spirit guide your celebrations. May the wisdom in these pages inspire you to cultivate a more profound reverence for our

Christian holidays, fostering gratitude, joy, and a greater sense of purpose.

I pray that as you embrace the lessons within this book, your holidays will become a time of spiritual renewal and profound connection with God. May you be encouraged to create meaningful traditions, cultivate a spirit of generosity, and share the love of Christ with others—both during the holiday season and throughout the year.

May this book be a source of blessing and inspiration as you embark on your journey to celebrate with purpose.

With heartfelt blessings,

Dr. Zolisha L Ware, ThD

Introduction

As Believers living in this fallen world, we certainly have the ability to transcend many barriers.

The most obvious barrier is having a thriving, living, vibrant relationship with the Father through our Lord and Savior Jesus, the Christ. We are saved from eternal damnation or eternal separation from God. Additionally, we are the benefactors of spiritual identity earned for us by our elder brother, Jesus the Christ. With all of that being said, being a Believer does not absolve any of us from storms, trials, and challenges. Storms, trials, and challenges are no more evident and their effects more pronounced than during the holiday season. Life is life for all: the Believer and the non-Believer in many ways. The holidays can exacerbate negative feelings of angst, anxiety, worry, depression, loneliness, etc. According to the American Psychological Association, 38% of the people surveyed said their stress increased during the holiday season, which can lead to physical illness, depression, anxiety, and substance misuse. In 2022, according to valuepenguin.com, a sizeable 55% of Americans were experiencing sadness and loneliness during the holidays, with a whopping 35% saying it was worse than the previous year. According to mentalhealthfirstaid.org, a 2020 survey found that 70% of people in the US reported feeling various degrees of loneliness heading into that holiday season- with more than 10% reporting extreme loneliness.

The objective of this book is not to diagnose a phenomenon that we all are aware of, but to be a source for the solution. The objective of this book is to be a valuable resource to which one can refer in order to facilitate one's own experience in such a way that one's holidays will be filled with peace (experiencing the peace of God), the love of God, the joy of the Lord, and contentment in one's circumstances regardless as to what one's reality may be. The truth of the matter is this: as Believers, we have the ability to transcend the effects of any experience.

This is one of the marks of Believers in this world. We can love the unlovely; we can be emotionally/physically whole and healed from trauma and physical disease; we can persevere during extremely difficult and challenging circumstances and situations in our lives. Being a Believer is so much more than a Sunday morning experience; it is an empowerment through Holy Spirit. Being a Believer is an enablement through Holy Spirit. It is my prayer that this book unlocks and represents to you some Kingdom truths and tools to which you have access. After you use these tools and apply these truths by the power of Holy Spirit, you will have HOLY GHOST HOLIDAY HELP and can go through your holiday season experiencing the love of God, peace of God, liberty, and joy of God through Holy Spirit. This topic certainly will not be exhausted in this first volume, of course. It will take several volumes and I'm not certain the topic will ever or can be exhausted.

This book is intended to be a resource to assist you during the holiday season. This book is the first installment of several volumes where I will expand on various topics regarding the matter of going through your holidays with an illumination of your identity in Christ, the peace of God, and the joy of the Lord. I know that this book will edify, strengthen, and fortify you because Holy Spirit told me that it would. Use it as a reference. Mark up the pages. Write in the columns. Let this book bring you some HOLY GHOST HOLIDAY HELP!

CHAPTER 1

Holy Ghost/ Holy Spirit

As Believers, Holy Spirit (or Holy Ghost) is OUR HELPER.

It does not matter to me what denominational affiliation you may have. Maybe in your denomination, you're unaccustomed to some of the nuances that are typical of my Pentecostal faith practice/experience. Maybe individuals with demonstrative praises or faith practices make you feel uncomfortable. Certainly, many who deem themselves Pentecostals in their expression of faith have been involved or perpetuated a lot of foolishness (in my opinion) in the name of being "Pentecostal." Beloved, I understand your stance. With that being said, if you've purchased this resource and are reading it, you are in NEED of some HOLY GHOST HOLIDAY HELP.

Just as our elder brother, Jesus has been controversial, misunderstood, and at times misrepresented, so has HOLY SPIRIT/HOLY GHOST unfortunately. However, if you are a Believer, you know that the foolishness of some in the name of being a Christian doesn't negate your experience with Jesus as a Believer. The same can be said of Holy Spirit.

Just because some have misinterpreted Holy Spirit does NOT negate the legitimacy of an experience with Him or of His function in our everyday lives. Furthermore, such representations do not stop Him from wanting to HELP YOU, regardless of your denominational lens. Holy Spirit is for every Catholic, Lutheran, Baptist, Methodist, and the list goes on. Empty religion will not help you when you're going through life's challenges and stressful seasons, but Holy Spirit will. While I consider myself inter-denominational, I appreciate all denominations. I believe all denominations/reformations have some things right and some things wrong. I don't believe God put all of His "eggs" in one "basket."

In the following Scriptures, He (Holy Spirit/ Holy Ghost) is interpreted from a Greek word, parakletos which means advocate, counsellor, or helper. So, when I say HOLY GHOST HOLIDAY HELP, it is indeed a SPECIAL type of assistance.

John 14:16

"And I will pray the Father, and he shall give you another Comforter, that he may abide with you forever"

John 14:26

"But the Comforter, which is the Holy Ghost, whom the Father will send in my name, he shall teach you all things, and bring all things to your remembrance, whatsoever I have said unto you."

John 15:26

"But when the Comforter is come, whom I will send unto you from the Father, even the Spirit of truth, which proceedeth from the Father, he shall testify of me."

John 16:7

"Nevertheless I tell you the truth; It is expedient for you that I go away: for if I go not away, the Comforter will not come unto you, but if I depart, I will send him unto you.

The truth of the matter is that life happens to us all. There are some things prayer can circumvent/prevent; I KNOW this fact as an intercessor. Everyone who passed (expires, dies, transitions), it wasn't their time. Every divorce that happens isn't the will of God. Every missed opportunity wasn't God closing a door. The intricacies of these occurrences are beyond the scope of this book but I do know that everything that happens in the Earth realm isn't necessarily sanctioned by God. God has given Believers the incredible tool of prayer to bring the will of God into the Earth realm through prayer and what I call para-prayer practices.

Some illnesses and diagnoses can be stopped by an anointed intercessor. Some relationships and connections can be saved or salvaged by an anointed intercessor. Some jobs and opportunities can manifest because of an anointed intercessor. Some plots and plans that the enemy has for individuals, territories, regions, etc, can be aborted by an anointed intercessor. Again, I won't get into all of that in this book since it's an assignment in a forthcoming book.

With that being said, prayer cannot prevent EVERYTHING from happening. Jesus told us in John 16:33 that we would have tribulation in this world. In Psalm 34:19, scripture teaches us that many are the afflictions of the righteous, but the Lord delivereth him out of them all.

It is important to note that our faith as Believers doesn't enable us to escape reality. Believers lose their jobs at times, get divorces, and receive unfavorable diagnoses. Believers are not exempt from life happening. So why be a Believer? Believers have Holy Spirit and all of His empowerment. Believers can stay "tapped in" (or aligned) with Holy Spirit. When Believers stay "tapped in" or aligned with Holy Spirit, we can not just endure, but thrive in a place of peace, joy, and identity in Christ. Remember, it is one of the defining characteristics of a Believer: the ability to TRANSCEND an experience through the person, power, and presence of Holy Spirit.

Holy Spirit is our help in difficult circumstances. Holy Spirit is our Help in challenging situations. Holy Spirit was given to us not just to allow us to have a demonstrative praise, but He IS our HELP! And the beauty of Holy Spirit is that He is not just helping us during the holiday season, but He is helping us ALL YEAR LONG. This is why I called this book Holy Ghost Holiday Help 365 Volume 1.

The thing about Holy Spirit is one has to be AWARE that He is available; one has to be OPEN to receive His assistance. Take a moment right now and ask Him to help you. Ask Him to show you as you're reading this book what to pray and how to pray. Believers can sometimes have a mindset of what we're going to do for God to prove our faith. It's a very easy trap to fall into: merit based living. When we truly live in the

Kingdom and cognizant of Kingdom principles, we understand that Holy Spirit doesn't need us to prove anything. The Father sent Holy Spirit to help us because the Father KNEW we'd need that help. So ask Him right now for His Help. Use your own words. There is no need to even close your eyes and kneel. You simply have to talk to Him. Tell Him that you are aware of His presence. Whether or not you feel Him doesn't matter to you. Tell Him that you need Him to help you through whatever your particular hardship is right now. Talk to Him! He is available TO YOU!

An extremely significant point to remember is that Holy Spirit is distinctive from you, your spirit, your soulish realm (which is made up of your thoughts, will, and emotions), your intuition, and your "first mind." Holy Spirit works THROUGH the aforementioned intangible parts of you because all of those parts came from your Heavenly Father. However, Holy Spirit is a different entity than those intangible parts of you. It's important to note that because a lot of times when Holy Spirit helps you, it may very well be counterintuitive or go against your soulish realm.

CHAPTER 2

You Have To Have A Made Up Mind

We have all heard that our mindset is extremely important as it relates to goal setting. As you're approaching the holiday season, it's important to have a mindset of I AM GOING TO GO THROUGH MY HOLIDAY SEASON WITH PEACE OF GOD, THE LOVE OF GOD

REIGNING IN MY SPIRIT, AND WITH THE JOY OF THE LORD. One must make up their mind at the onset of what their holiday experience is going to be. We cannot wait to see how we feel and then decide how we're going to respond to our feelings. This is a huge mistake that a lot of Believers make. We must decide how our experience is going to be BEFORE our feelings even get "a vote" in the matter. We know that the enemy seeks to steal, kill, and destroy us (John 10:10). Most committed Christians, regardless of denomination, have a firm resolve on their believing faith. In other words, the enemy can't necessarily steal their salvation. I submit to you though that the enemy can certainly steal from committed Believers. The enemy can steal your faith that your life will ever get better. The enemy can steal your hope that you can survive a diagnosis that is not ideal. The enemy can steal your belief that strained and even estranged relationships can be healed and restored as if the infraction, wound, etc., never happened. Don't let him steal from you!

You'd be surprised at how POWERFUL your mind is. Scripture teaches us in Romans 7:25

that we serve God with our minds. The word mind in this text of Scripture comes from the Greek word voi, which means understanding and reason (origin is nous). So you see Beloved, your mind is "prime real estate,' so to speak. As realtors and entrepreneurs often say – LOCATION, LOCATION, LOCATION!

It's important to note that your mind is not comprised only of your brain and thoughts, but it is also comprised of your heart posture. This book addresses thoughts and I'd also like to address heart posture as it relates to your mind in future volumes of this book.

Are you willing to have a great holiday season? Is it your desire to come through your holiday season with joy and peace? Have you divorced yourself from any desire to garner pity and or attention because of what you're going through?

John 5:1-23 gives an account of an impotent man that was in his condition for thirty eight years, waiting for the water to be troubled in order for him to receive his healing. Jesus didn't respond to him by giving him pity. Jesus didn't blame others for not helping him to the pool. Jesus didn't give him a hug, "pet him up" and heal him. I used to think it was rather insensitive, but Jesus asked the man if he was willing to be made whole before He healed him.

Beloveds, sometimes we like the pity that our situations and circumstances give us. Sometimes, we enjoy the emotional rush of getting attention, empathy, and understanding from other individuals. While there is nothing inherently wrong with being stroked or soothed emotionally during times of distress, it can become a crutch that impedes our forward progress. For example, if you got a divorce this year, you're definitely still in pain. With that being said, thirty eight years after a divorce, you should've certainly gotten to a place of healing and wholeness and made steps to move forward in your life.

Another example is grief over the passing of a family member, friend, or loved one. Certainly when we lose someone close to us, such as parent, child, close friend, etc., our lives are never the same. In a lot of ways, there is a void that will always be present, even as Believers. This is a completely healthy phenomenon. With that being said, grief should not cripple the Believer for decades at a time. The Believer can grieve in a healthy manner and not allow what I call the "Spirit of Grief" to get on them.

In our text in John 5, Jesus loved the impotent man so much, that He addressed the root cause. I love how our Jesus cuts right to the chase! He said simply, do you WANT to be made whole? He asked Him if this is what He wanted. Beloved, do you WANT to go through your holidays and subsequently your life with an illumination of your identity in Christ, experiencing the peace of God, and enjoying the joy of the Lord? Or do you prefer to remain stuck, stagnant, depressed, and pitiful? The choice is yours.

CHAPTER 3

The Enemy Is A Thief And A Liar

The enemy can steal a Believer's joy and hope. The enemy can steal a Believer's revelation of their identity in Christ and the love that the Father has for them. The enemy can steal the experience of knowing that they are not alone, but

Holy Spirit is always with them. Remember that the devil is a liar, according to John 8:44.

One of the biggest lies that he tells the Believer is that they are all alone. The enemy lies to the Believer and tells them that no one loves them or cares. Maybe you're reading this and you don't have a lot of friends in the natural. Maybe you're reading this and you are estranged from family members or loved ones. Maybe you're experiencing a high level of betrayal, etc.

One of the biggest lies the enemy will tell you is NO ONE is with you. The devil is a complete, comprehensive liar! It doesn't matter who has let you down or disappointed you. That's them, but God is God! The enemy will try to convince you that you are alone. This is a lie according to Matthew 28:18. Jesus said, "Lo, I am with you always, even until the end of the world." Beloved, you and I MUST internalize the Word of God. Scripture MUST become part of your spiritual DNA so that when the enemy comes to you with a lie, and he will, you have something for Holy Spirit to use AGAINST him! Recite the Word of God out loud when the enemy lies to you! Holy Spirit will always back up the Word! Hallelujah!

CHAPTER 4

Combat Thoughts With Words

A Believer cannot be lazy. Even though Christ gave us victory over all of the enemy's authority in this world, we have to use our delegated authority (or exousia) to keep the enemy in his place, which is under our feet. If you think he's just going to lay down and let you "skip through the tulips" so to speak and just give you victory, you're sadly mistaken. Particularly when the enemy has had a stronghold or a foothold in an area of your life for a long time, he is not going to give up that territory easily. And you've got to be okay with that. You can be okay with that when you understand that his desires and intentions for your life MEAN NOTHING.

The Father has made you a king and priest over your life! God has given you authority to legislate and establish in your life according to His will. According to Proverbs 18:21, death and life are in the power of your tongue. What does that mean practically? When you feel feelings of loneliness, isolation, depression want to sweep over you, SAY OUT OF YOUR MOUTH....NO!!! If you have to do this several times daily, DO IT! REPEAT WHAT THE WORD SAYS ABOUT YOU. ACTUALLY SAY OUT OF YOUR MOUTH.... ACCORDING TO MATTHEW 28:18, JESUS IS WITH ME RIGHT NOW. ALSO, I HAVE THE POWER AND PRESENCE OF HOLY SPIRIT WITH ME RIGHT NOW. I AM NOT ALONE!!

I believe in Jesus and therapy. If you have any sort of mental health diagnosis, please follow your counselor's, psychiatrist's, or psychologist's recommendations. If you have been prescribed medication to assist you, please take your medication. Just as I'd encourage a diabetic to take their insulin and to check their blood sugar; just as I'd instruct an individual who fell from their bike and broke their arm to go to the hospital to get their broken bone reset; just as I'd run to get an AEP device to assist an individual in the middle of a heart attack and then call 911 as I'm praying.

For those with mental health disorders, I admonish you to take your medication. Prayer works. Intercession is my first ministry love. I knew I was an intercessor before I knew I was a preacher. Mental health issues doesn't necessarily mean anything demonic is going on. It can mean there is a physiological problem going on. I saw a quote on social media that says it best.... prayer deals with the demon, but therapy deals with the trauma. If you've experienced certain types of trauma, such as divorce, the death of a loved one, the murder of a loved one, childhood abuse, or neglect, please see a mental health professional. I've said for years and will continue to say that if you think you need therapy, you probably do. Unfortunately, there is such a negative stigma associated with mental health issues. The enemy uses this stigma to keep so many Believers in bondage. Don't let that devil do it to you another day. Seek professional help if that's what you feel you need. There is no shame in that. You can be a Believer "to the bone" and still greatly benefit from professional mental health counseling or medication for a mental health disorder.

CHAPTER 5

Accept Your Reality

One of the first steps to being healthy and whole, even during the holidays, is to accept your reality. Maybe you've gone through a divorce this year; accept that the marriage is over. Maybe you were fired from a job that you really loved and enjoyed; accept that that job is not in your life anymore. Maybe you've experienced a betrayal so deep that your head is still spinning. Accept that that connection/relationship/friendship is over.

Maybe you've had a diagnosis that is not ideal. Walking in faith and working your faith is not carte blanche to deny your reality. Acknowledge your diagnosis as a fact before you begin to fight the good fight of faith.

As Believers, we appropriate our faith for our real life challenges, circumstances, and situations. As psychologically healthy individuals, we do not deny reality. We depend on our faith to overcome our challenges, to transcend them, not to deny them.

Divorce Yourself From Unrealistic Expectations

If you haven't fostered great relationships, don't expect your family or friends to have "gooey" feelings for you just because it's the holidays. Rome wasn't built in a day and neither are healthy strong, connections.

Your Finances Are What They Are

Make up in your mind that you are not going to go broke trying to give gifts that you cannot afford. Let all of your friends and family members know that this year, it's not wise for me to spend my money on gifts. Individuals who truly love you don't put expectations on you for gifts.

Maybe you can't have an elaborate Thanksgiving or Christmas meal this year due to financial challenges; don't despair. Be open about it and decide not to stress out about such a trivial matter.

Those with children (or without children) can more often get some help from social service organizations or charities. Explain to your children that though you're going through a financial challenge now, things won't always be in this state. Times of financial challenge is an excellent time to consider making gifts or giving gifts of sentimental or practical value. For example, gift someone with a promise to babysit for them, do some yard work, or clean up their house. Holy Spirit will give you creative ways to be a blessing without finances.

CHAPTER 8

Get Yourself Off Of Your Mind

Something that has proven in my life to be an effective strategy is to get myself off of my mind during times of depression and isolation. While we certainly want to ask Holy Spirit to give us an audit of our challenges so that we can have clarity, we do not want to remain STUCK mentally. One way that we can get ourselves off of our minds is to intentionally be a blessing to someone else. This is counter intuitive, but it works. How do you do it? First, ask Holy Spirit who you can be a blessing to during the holidays. Holy Spirit is so creative and He will open your spiritual eyes to those in your sphere to which you can be a blessing.

Here are some examples:

- Volunteer at the hospital.
- Volunteer at an assisted living facility.
- Meet a practical need of someone in your neighborhood, such as babysitting or helping them clean their house.
- Call a local school and pay for children's lunch that is past due if it's in your budget to do so.

CHAPTER 9

Guard Your Gates

You and I cannot digest any and everything and maintain our place of peace and joy. For example, if you've gone through a painful breakup, why listen to sad love songs for hours on end? It's difficult enough to get over it, so why exacerbate those feelings by feeding them sad love songs?

If you've lost someone, why watch movies about a loved one dying? Granted, sometimes, it may be therapeutic watching others go through similar experiences. With that being said, it can turn from being therapeutic to being a metaphoric door that the enemy uses to hinder you if you're not careful.

Remember, whatever you feed will grow. You and I cannot feed negative thoughts or emotions. It is an opportunity for the enemy of our souls to slip in, further damage us, and hinder our forward progress.

CHAPTER 10

Watch Your Tongue

It is EXTREMELY important to speak life. Even as you're speaking of your situation, always leave a conversation about it and its negativity on a "high note." Always speak words of faith and not defeat. Do not speak out of your frustrations and out of your emotions. This is easier said than done. With that being said, it must be done in order to secure victory. Speaking life gives Holy Spirit space to work and to answer your prayers.

Don't pray for victory, declare victory, decree victory, then speak defeat or constantly rehearse what's wrong. It gives the enemy space and is counter productive to your forward progress. For example, if you have a child or loved one who is battling an addiction and they do something that is completely opposite of what you are believing God to manifest in their life, DO NOT pray all morning and then speak incessantly about their most recent infraction in the afternoon. Proverbs 18:21 states that death and life is in the power of your tongue.

Make a decision and ask Holy Spirit for help to assist you in keeping a close "eye" on the words that you speak. Maybe it is not the enemy but your own words that are hindering the desired result for your specific situation.

CHAPTER 11

Speak In Your Heavenly Language

I recognize that every Believer reading this book is not Pentecostal in their faith expression. For those of us who are, I recommend you speaking in your Heavenly language for 10-15 minutes daily. Scripture teaches in Jude verse 20 that when we pray in Holy Ghost, we build up our most holy faith. When you're battling depression, feelings of angst, anxiety and loneliness, your faith muscle must be built up. Build it up by circumventing your intellect and praying in your Heavenly language or tongues. The Bible says that when you speak in an unknown tongue that your spirit is speaking directly to God (See I Corinthians 4:4 &14). Allow Holy Spirit to move in your life by using the precious gift of speaking in tongues on a regular basis.

I highly recommend my spiritual father's book, DECLOAKING THE HOLY GHOST (by Dr. Larry Barnett) to learn more about the phenomenon of Holy Spirit baptism.

CHAPTER 12

Increase Your Devotion

Ideally, one doesn't want to wait until they're in a battle to get prepared. This is why our daily place of devotion in our lives is of paramount significance. Set aside time to pray, fast, worship, and commune with God. That personal devotion is a place of strength in your life and gives Holy Spirit space to work on your behalf.

CHAPTER 13

Tend To Your Natural Man

Maybe it's not the devil. Maybe you just need to get some quality rest. Maybe you would not be so anxious if you had a more still, quiet environment. Are you overstimulated? Do you sleep with your television on? Do you sleep with your cell phone right by your bed and every time a notification goes off you hear it? Granted, most adults have responsibilities and must be reachable. With that being said, the world will survive if you turn off your notifications to get a good night's rest. If, God forbid, something tragic happens, individuals can always come to your house or leave a voice mail message. The world will survive without you being available to anyone outside of your spouse for a few hours.

CHAPTER 14

Walk In The Light And In Light

Something as simple as getting enough sunlight can help greatly assist you as well as you're navigating through your holiday season. Experts suggest 10-30 minutes of sunlight daily. Most experts agree that simply sitting by a window doesn't do the job. In order to get the Vitamin

D that the sun provides, one must actually be outside. So, pull open those curtains AND take a walk around your block. You'd be surprised how fresh air and some sunshine will do for you.

CHAPTER 15

Who Is Truly The Reason For The Season?

As Believers, we must recognize who is truly the reason for the season. Surely, the holidays have been commercialized. Additionally, Jesus wasn't born in December anyways either. Certainly, a great portion of our holiday festivities have pagan roots and origins. With all of that being said,

I LOVE THE HOLIDAYS, as do most individuals. If you are a Believer, it is a time of year that should be dedicated to remembering and being especially aware of WHY our Savior came into the world, which was to die for our sins. I'm all for giving and getting gifts. I'm all for cooking and enjoying great meals. I'm all for the festive decorations and the like. With that being said, Christmas is not about ANY of the trappings or accouterments to which we have ascribed it. Christmas, simply put, is about Christ. Keep Him at the forefront of your mind and thoughts, particularly if you're having a difficult time. The enemy LOVES to distract us, but when we remain focused on Christ, it becomes a more difficult task for the enemy to distract us.

CHAPTER 16

Righteousness Peace And Joy In The Holy Ghost-Your Kingdom Posture

Many Believers attend church and are very active in their faith community but never get around to learning who they are IN CHRIST.

Romans 14:17 tells us that the Kingdom of God isn't about what you wear or eat. The Kingdom of God isn't about what's tangible. Paul told us that the Kingdom of God is righteousness, peace, and joy in Holy Ghost. So, it doesn't matter what type of car you drive if you don't have righteousness, peace, and joy in Holy Ghost. The square footage of your home doesn't matter if you don't have righteousness, peace, and joy in Holy Ghost. It doesn't matter how much education you have, how popular or well thought of you may be, or if you've reached your goal weight, if you don't have righteousness, peace, and joy in Holy Ghost.

The interesting thing is that the Kingdom of God is within us according to Jesus Luke 17:21. Therefore, no matter what challenges you are facing during this holiday season, you can always tap into your identity (righteousness) and your benefits (peace and joy) because they are in the Holy Ghost.

Let's go deeper.

Romans 14:17 says, "For the kingdom of God is not meat and drink; but righteousness, and peace, and joy in the Holy Ghost."

The word "righteousness" in this text comes from the Greek word dikalos, which means justice, righteous, or just. It occurs 92 times in the entire Bible and in 85 verses. It is equity of the character of God especially Christian justification. The phenomenon of justification is a foundation in our Christian faith. Justification or to justify is the action of declaring or making righteous in the sight of God. So, when Paul states that the kingdom of God is righteousness, peace, and joy in the Holy Ghost in Romans 14:17, he lists righteousness, which speaks directly to the Believer's identity.

If you are going to have Holy Ghost Holiday Help 365, you need to internalize the truth that God sent Jesus to suffer and die on the Cross to procure justification on your behalf. You have been made righteous by the blood of Jesus as an individual who has accepted Christ into your heart as your Lord and Savior. So, if you've had a moral failure or the ending of a relationship connection has been your fault, simply repent (I John 1:8-10) and ask God how you can make it right with the individual. If you're going into the holiday season and the squandering of an opportunity was your fault and you're tempted this holiday season to get into condemnation while lamenting over poor choices and past sins. DO NOT DO that! Simply repent, and ask God to give you STRATEGY on how to recover or ask Him for another opportunity. Quite frankly, it is much harder to forgive yourself and to let yourself "off of the hook" than it is for God to forgive us. The enemy is an opportunist and will leave any metaphoric door that you leave open.

Romans 8:1 states that those who walk in the Spirit have no condemnation (paraphrase). The enemy will attempt to use the spirit of condemnation to keep you stuck on that metaphoric hamster wheel of condemnation to steal (John 10:10) the fullness of pleasure from you during the holiday season. Do not allow him to do it! Repent of any poor choices that you may have made, and receive God's forgiveness. Next, ask Him for strategy to make things right in any relationships or connections that are the will of God for your life. God is a Restorer and will certainly give you another chance if it's in His will for your life. If He doesn't give you another chance with a particular relationship, connection, or opportunity, surely you can learn a valuable lesson as you continue to move forward with your life. You must internalize Romans 8:28, which states that all things do work together for the good of those who love the Lord and are called according to His purpose (paraphrase).

In Romans 14:17, the word peace comes from the Greek word "eirene" which means complete or whole. It means the same as the Hebrew word, shalom, in the Old Testament. Completeness and wholeness in Holy Spirit are a part of your Kingdom inheritance. Notice, it's not predicated upon whether your circumstances or situation in your life are ideal. Maybe you went through a divorce this year. Maybe you lost a job and are financially struggling during this holiday season. Maybe your children (or parents) are estranged from you during this holiday season.

Maybe you have a diagnosis that is not favorable that is looming over your head during this holiday season. All of these scenarios are certainly real life situations and circumstances that can cause angst, anxiety, despair, etc.

Beloved, you can "tap in" to Holy Spirit and receive His peace. Say out of your mouth, "Holy Spirit, I receive your peace. I am not going to worry or have anxiety about thus and so." Beloved, we must be proactive in our Christian faith as we are applying principles of victorious Christian living. Having and walking in victory is going to certainly REQUIRE your participation. A powerful Scripture to quote during times of decreeing and declaring peace in Holy Spirit over your life is John 14:27, which states: "Peace I leave with you, my peace I give unto you: not as the world giveth, give I unto you. Let not your heart be troubled, neither let it be afraid."

This text states plainly and with much clarity that peace is your portion! Regardless as to any circumstance or situation that is not ideal that may be going on in your life, the peace that Christ gave you and peace in Holy Ghost TRANSCENDS all of that. Again, as Believers, we don't deny our reality. Instead, we submit ourselves to the Word of God and to the Person of Holy Spirit.

In Romans 14:17, joy in the Holy Ghost is listed as part of the Believer's inheritance. The word joy in that text comes from the Greek word "chara" which means delight or gladness. Holy Spirit will truly make you lightheaded, regardless as to what's going on in your life. Have you ever had a day that something "heavy" was going on in your life, but you spent time with God in prayer, meditation, and the Word and simply forgot about it? Maybe a bill was due and you did your due diligence but were unable to get the money to pay the bill. Or maybe a child or grandchild of yours was in a situation that could have caused you stress as a parent or grandparent, but you gave it to God in your time with God and you literally forgot about it.

As you go through your holiday season, Holy Spirit wants to give you His joy, and He wants to give you His gladness and delight. Our bodies were not made to carry severe emotional weight and burden long term. I truly believe lots of sicknesses and diseases are manifested this very way. So, cast your care according to I Peter 5:7 and allow Holy Spirit to give you His peace.

Of course, I'm not saying to cast your responsibility. Do what you can do or what's in your ability to do to get a favorable outcome. Going back to the bill needing to be paid example, contact the creditor and see if an extension can be given. See if you're able to get a second job or if you're able to earn more money in order to take care of a bill. In other words, do your part. Having said all of that Beloveds, what else can you do? You certainly cannot worry a bill into being paid.

About The Author

Valencia Clark graduated salutatorian of her Meridian High School Class of 1995 in Mounds, IL. She received her Bachelor of Arts degree in Speech Communication from the University of Illinois at Urbana/Champaign in 2000. She received Christ as her Savior in 1996. She received her call to ministry in 1998/1999 while under "watch care" at the Church of the Living God – Pillar and Ground of the Truth (affectionately known as "Love Corner") in Champaign, IL under the leadership of the Honorable Bishop Lloyd E. Gwin. While at Love Corner, Valencia developed a love for service and for the Word of God. Valencia served in various capacities and developed lifelong connections while in undergrad attending Love Corner.

After she graduated college, the Lord spoke to Valencia and told her to move back home and to help her Pastor build the local church. Valencia did that for over two decades. Valencia received her ministry licensing and ordination credentials from her spiritual father, the Honorable Apostle Larry T. Barnett, Sr. (St. John Praise and Worship Center, SJPWC, in Pulaski, IL. Dr. Barnett is the Assistant to Bishop Ron Webb of Covenant Ministries, Poplar Bluff, MO). While at SJPWC, Valencia served as an associate minister of the Gospel, the first Director of SJPWC Preparatory Academy, a praise team member, a choir member, intercessory ministry, administrative assistant to the Pastor, Communication Ministry member, elected the first President of Kerusso Logos (SJPWC's organization for associate ministers), chairperson of various programs/events, and was hand selected by her spiritual father to chair SJPWC's evangelistic "arm," - TAKING IT TO THE STREETS.

Her ministry graces/assignments are pastor, intercessor, prophet, and Bible teacher. Intercession is her "first ministry love." Valencia is the founder of A SPECIAL TOUCH OUTREACH MINISTRIES and makes her home in Las Vegas, NV. Her Pastor is the Honorable Apostle Zolisha L. Ware, founder of Fearless Fire Global Transformation Center/Fearless Fire Network in Bloomington-Normal, IL.

Index

I

illnesses, 9
individuals, 5, 9, 16, 26, 39, 44
infraction, 14, 35
inheritance, 49, 51
insensitive, 16
insulin, 23
intangible, 11
intercessor, 8, 9, 23, 55
intuition, 11
isolation, 22, 30

J

Jesus, 1, 6, 9, 15, 16, 17, 19, 23, 43, 46, 47
joy, 3, 4, 10, 15, 17, 18, 32, 46, 47, 51

K

Kingdom, 3, 11, 45, 46, 49

L

lazy, 21